CONTENTS

KV-618-825

CHAPTER 1

THE HUMAN Body

Tooth enamel is the hardest part of the body. Speaking one word takes dozens of **muscles**. Humans shed their skin. Hearts are electric. The body lets people think, walk, talk and feel. The human body is amazing!

BRIGHT IDEA BOOKS

YOUR Nose NEVER STOPS Growing: COOL HUMAN BODY FACTS

by Kimberly M. Hutmacher

Raintree is an imprint of Capstone Global Library Limited, a company incorporated in England and Wales having its registered office at 264 Banbury Road, Oxford, OX2 7DY – Registered company number: 6695582

www.raintree.co.uk
myorders@raintree.co.uk

Edited by Meg Gaertner
Designed by Becky Daum
Production by Colleen McLaren
Printed and bound in India

ISBN 978 1 4747 7456 7 (hardback)
ISBN 978 1 4747 8241 8 (paperback)

British Library Cataloguing in Publication Data
A full catalogue record for this book is available from the British Library.

Acknowledgements
We would like to thank the following for permission to reproduce photographs: iStockphoto: adventtr, 8–9, chombosan, 23, gisele, 16–17, Gmint, 26, Lokibaho, 5, RapidEye, cover, tzahiV, 18; Shutterstock Images: Anton Nalivayk, 15, Avatar_023, 21, Jin young-in, 10, kaling2100, 8, Kawitsara, 11, Larysa Ray, 30–31, meow wii, 16, Mouy_Photo, 18–19, patrisyu, 7, Sebastian Kaulitzki, 25, 28, Valentyna Chukhlyebova, 13
Every effort has been made to contact copyright holders of material reproduced in this book. Any omissions will be rectified in subsequent printings if notice is given to the publisher.

We would like to thank Melissa Bates, PhD, Assistant Professor of Health and Human Physiology, for her help with this book.

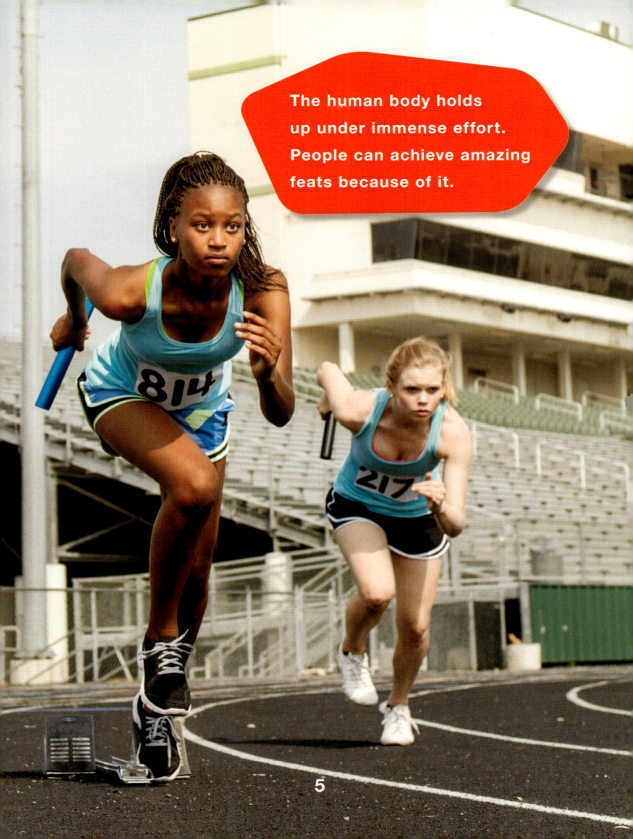

The human body holds up under immense effort. People can achieve amazing feats because of it.

CHAPTER 2

FRAME

The adult **skeleton** has 206 bones. They make the body's frame. Humans have more bones as babies. The bones join together over time. Almost all the bones are connected to each other. Only one bone is not. It is the hyoid bone in the throat. This bone supports the tongue.

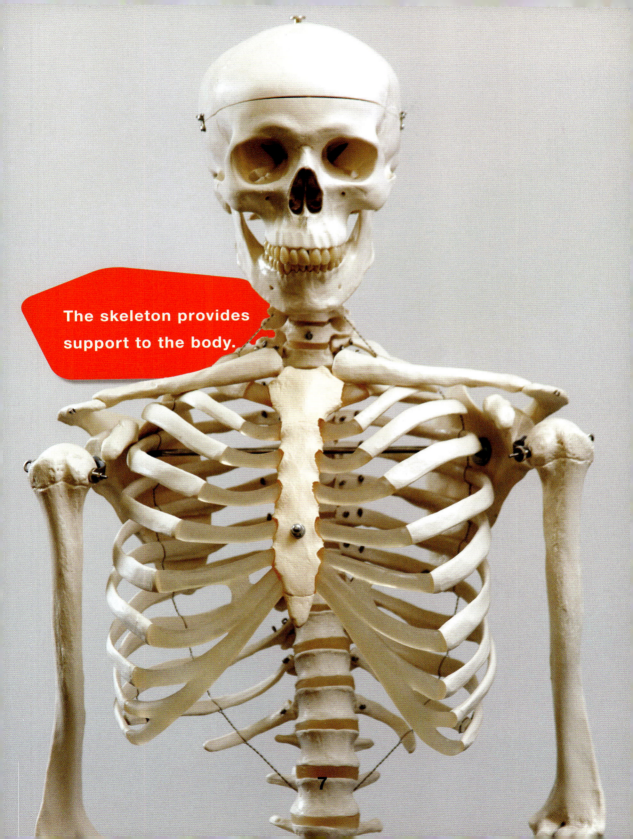

The skeleton provides support to the body.

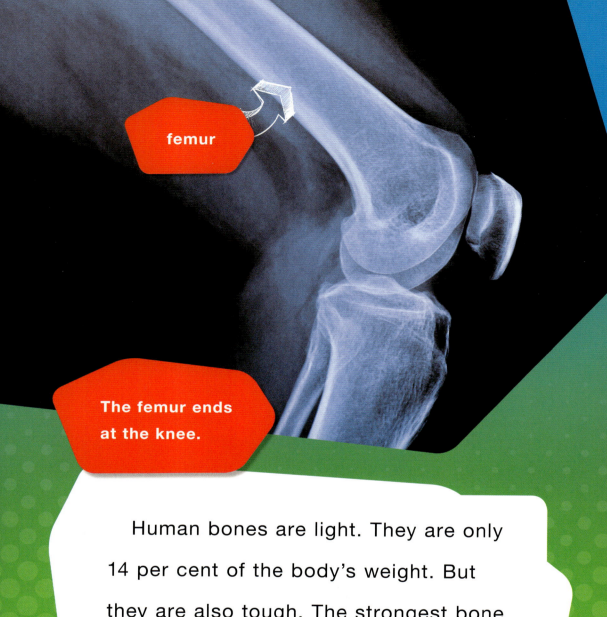

femur

The femur ends at the knee.

Human bones are light. They are only 14 per cent of the body's weight. But they are also tough. The strongest bone is the femur. This is the long bone in the thigh. It is as strong as concrete.

STRONG BITE

Bones are not the hardest part of the body. The hardest part is tooth enamel.

Teeth have enamel on the outside. They also have long roots that can only be seen in an X-ray.

roots

The face has 15 bones. But two features are not made of bone. The outer ear and the outer nose are made of **cartilage**. **Gravity** pulls on the cartilage. It sags over time. It looks bigger as people age.

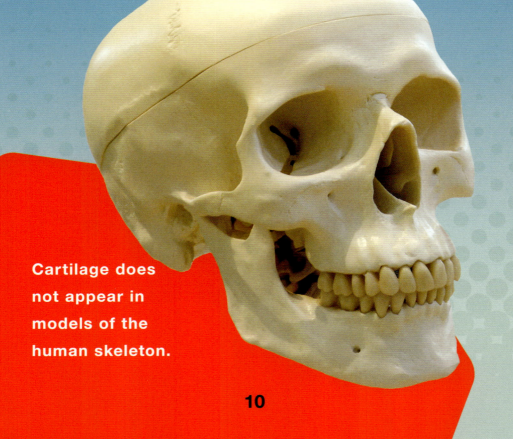

Cartilage does not appear in models of the human skeleton.

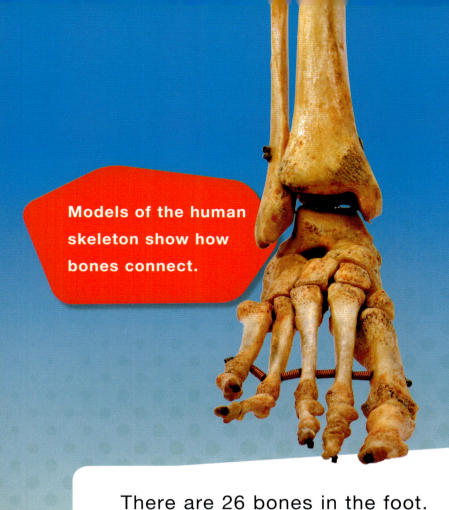

There are 26 bones in the foot. The average shoe size is increasing. In the UK, it has increased by two sizes since 1970. The average woman's foot is now a size 6. The average man's foot is a size 10.

CHAPTER 3

MOVEMENT

Humans have more than 600 muscles. They help the body to move. People use 200 muscles to take one step! It takes 72 muscles to speak one word. The smallest muscle is inside the ear. The longest muscle runs from the hip to the knee.

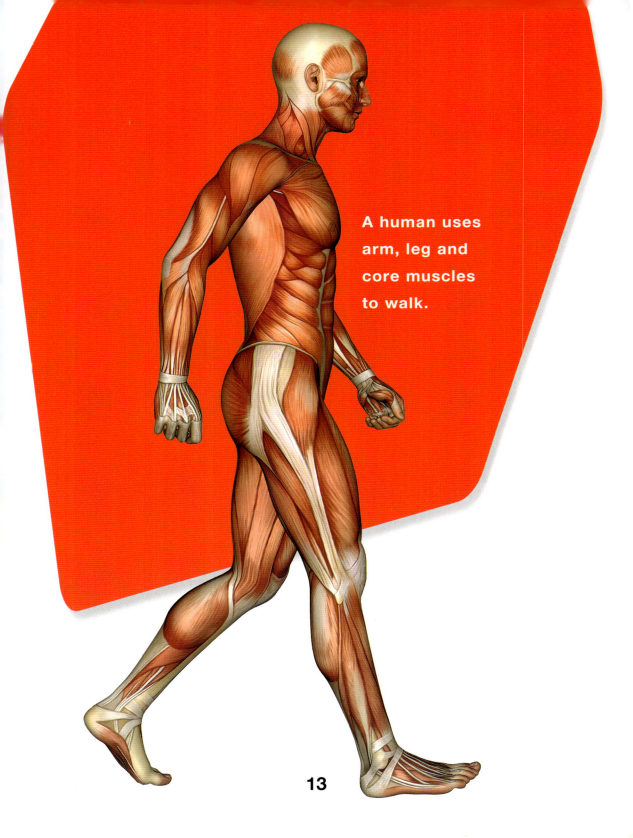

A human uses
arm, leg and
core muscles
to walk.

13

CHAPTER 4

OUTSIDE

Skin is the largest human **organ**. It protects the body. Skin is thinnest on the eyelids. It is thickest on the heels. Humans shed 30,000 to 40,000 skin **cells** per minute. New skin cells grow. A new top layer grows about once each month.

Skin has many layers. The top layer of skin rubs off as cells die.

epidermis layers

dermis

hypodermis

NAILS

Fingernails are tools. They help people pick things up. They help people scratch an itch. It takes about six months to grow a fingernail from the nail bed to fingertip. Fingernails grow two to three times as fast as toenails. The nail on a child's middle finger grows the fastest. Nails also grow faster during the summer.

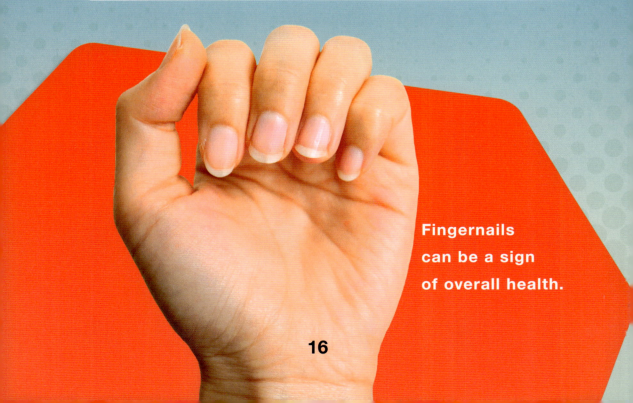

Fingernails can be a sign of overall health.

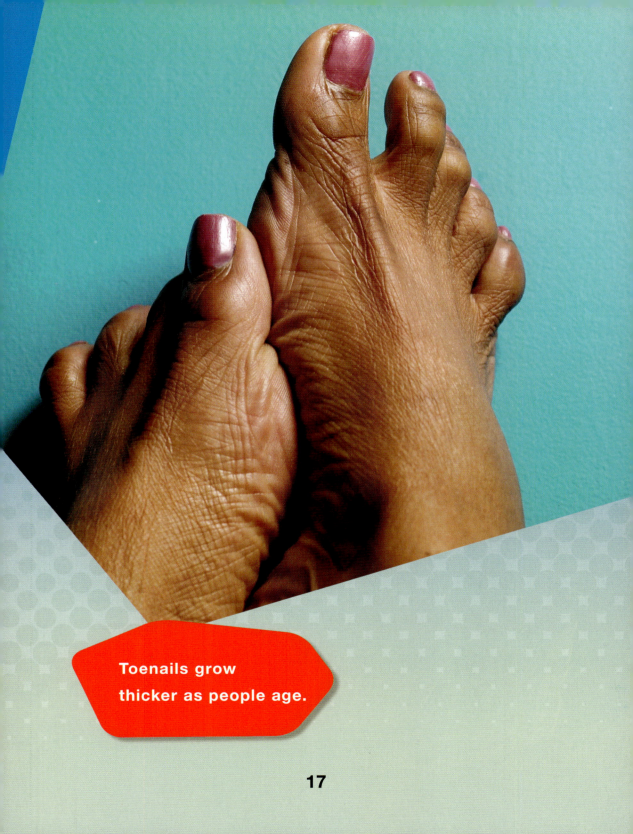

Toenails grow
thicker as people age.

HAIR

An adult has more than five million hairs. About 100,000 of these are on the head. A woman's hair grows slower than a man's hair. Humans lose up to 100 hairs a day.

Hair keeps the body warm. When it is cold, the muscles around each hair **contract**. Goosebumps form.

Goosebumps make the hair stand up.

CHAPTER 5

INSIDE

What do computers and human hearts have in common? They are electric! The heart beats because of electrical signals. It beats 60 to 100 times per minute. This is about 100,000 times a day. The heart is about the size of a fist. A man's heart is 280 to 340 grams (10 to 12 ounces). A woman's heart weighs less. The heart pumps about 5.7 litres (10 pints) of blood each minute.

BABY BEATS

A baby's heart beats faster than an adult's heart.

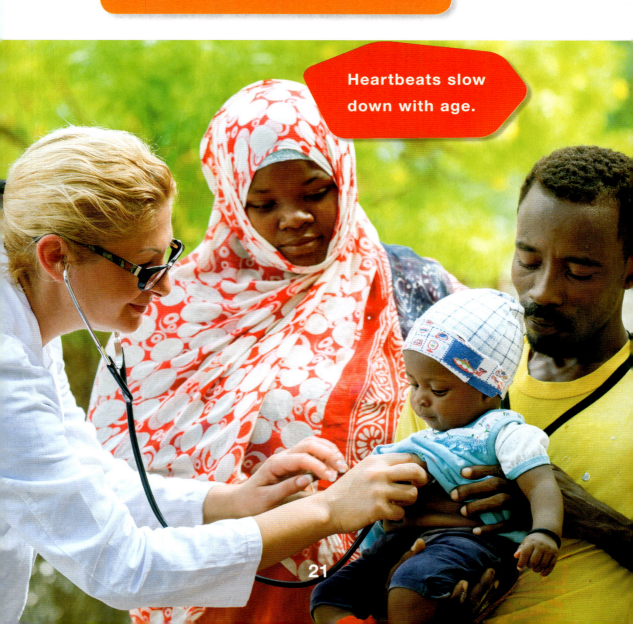

Heartbeats slow down with age.

STOMACH

The stomach can stretch. It can hold 2 to 4 litres (3.5 to 7 pints) of food.

Acid in the stomach breaks down food.

Stomachs are always making noises. Empty stomachs make a growling sound.

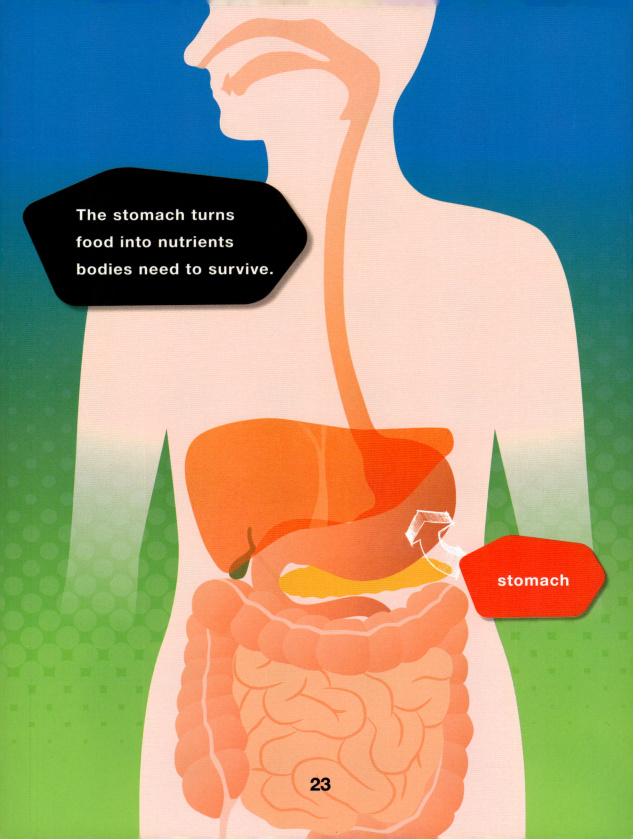

The stomach turns food into nutrients bodies need to survive.

stomach

BRAIN

The brain controls the body. But it weighs only about 1.6 kilograms (3.5 pounds). About 73 per cent of the brain is water. The brain changes based on how it is used.

ACTIVE SLEEP

A brain sleeps. But brain activity never stops. A brain is even more active at night.

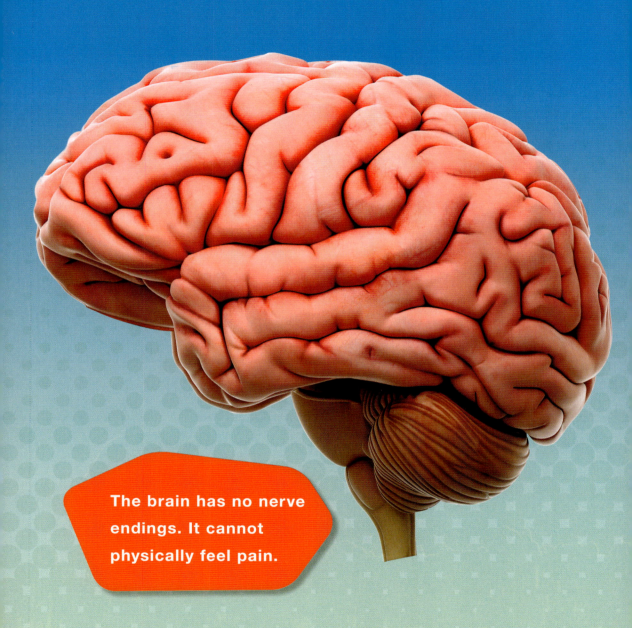

The brain has no nerve endings. It cannot physically feel pain.

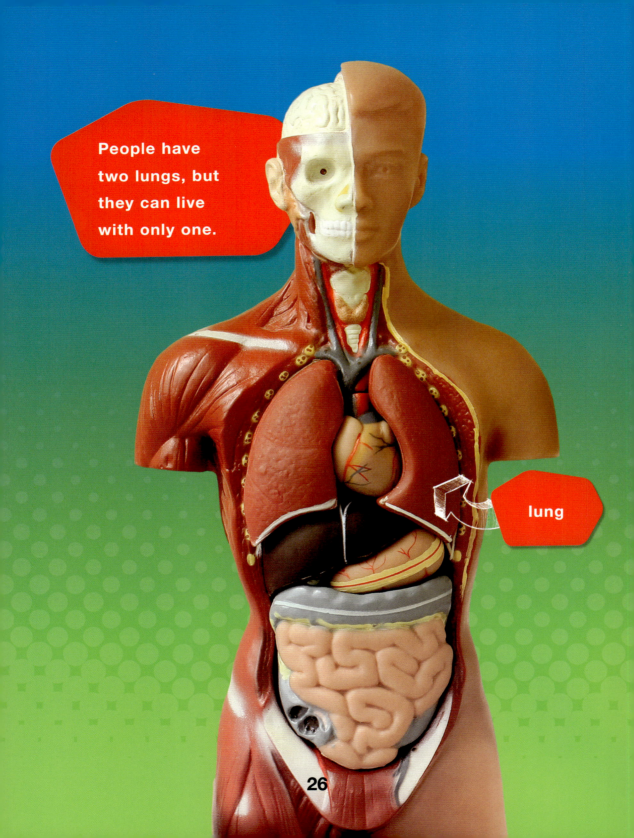

People have two lungs, but they can live with only one.

lung

LUNGS

Lungs help the body breathe. Lungs are light. They are filled with millions of air sacs. These sacs would cover five parking spaces if spread out. Humans breathe about 6 litres (13 pints) of air every minute. Women and children breathe faster than men.

GLOSSARY

cartilage
firm, flexible tissue

cell
the smallest basic unit of all living things

contract
to become shorter and tighter

gravity
the force that attracts the body towards the centre of the Earth

lung
one of two organs in the chest used for breathing

muscle
body tissue that can contract and make movement

organ
an independent part of the body that carries out one or more special functions

skeleton
the framework of bones that supports a body

tooth enamel
the visible part of a tooth

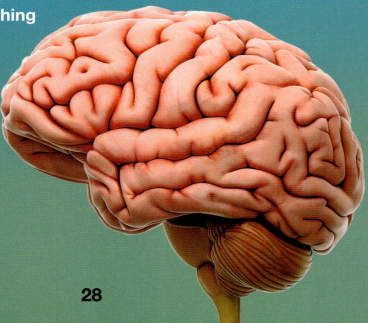

TRIVIA

1. An adult makes about 0.9 litres (1.5 pints) of sweat each day.

2. The average person makes 1.4 litres (3 pints) of gas each day.

3. Human eyes blink about 15 times per minute.

4. Humans make 0.9 to 1.9 litres (1.5 to 4 pints) of spit each day.

5. Belly button lint is made up of body hair, dead skin cells and clothing fibres.

ACTIVITY

FINGERPRINT FUN!

Fingerprints are fully formed even before birth. No two sets of fingerprints are alike. Even identical twins have different fingerprints. Do you want to see your own fingerprints? To do so, follow these steps:

1. Trace your hand onto a piece of white paper.

2. Draw a thick layer of pencil on another piece of paper.

3. One at a time, rub each fingertip into the layer of pencil. Then press firmly onto the correct finger on the other paper. This can also be done using an inkpad. Just make sure the ink is washable. Compare your prints to your friends' prints.

FIND OUT MORE

Ready to learn even more amazing facts about the human body? Check out these resources.

Books

Human Body (Science Lab), Anna Claybourne (Silver Dolphin Books, 2019)

Utterly Amazing Human Body, Robert Winston (DK, 2015)

Totally Wacky Facts about the Human Body, Cari Meister (Raintree, 2017)

Websites

DK Find Out!
www.dkfindout.com/uk/human-body/

BBC Bitesize: Human Body
www.bbc.com/bitesize/topics/zcyycdm

INDEX